essays and dissertations made easy

Hazel Hutchison

flash.

...cation

...on Road, London NW1 3BH.

...r Education is an Hachette UK company

...st published in UK 2011 by Hodder Education.

Copyright © 2011 Hazel Hutchison

British Library Cataloguing in Publication Data: a catalogue record for this title
is available from the British Library.

10 9 8 7 6 5 4 3 2 1

The publisher has used its best endeavours to ensure that any website
addresses referred to in this book are correct and active at the time of going
to press. However, the publisher and the author have no responsibility for the
websites and can make no guarantee that a site will remain live or that the
content will remain relevant, decent or appropriate.

The publisher has made every effort to mark as such all words which it
believes to be trademarks. The publisher should also like to make it clear that
the presence of a word in the book, whether marked or unmarked, in no way
affects its legal status as a trademark.

Every reasonable effort has been made by the publisher to trace the copyright
holders of material in this book. Any errors or omissions should be notified in
writing to the publisher, who will endeavour to rectify the situation for any
reprints and future editions.

Hachette UK's policy is to use papers that are natural, renewable and
recyclable products and made from wood grown in sustainable forests.
The logging and manufacturing processes are expected to conform to the
environmental regulations of the country of origin.

www.hoddereducation.co.uk

Typeset by MPS Limited, a Macmillan Company.
Printed in Great Britain by CPI Cox & Wyman, Reading.

Contents

Introduction   2

1   **Before you begin**   4

2   **Know your assignment**   12

3   **Questions and topics**   24

4   **Finding the right material**   30

5   **Planning and structure**   36

6   **Introductions and conclusions**   42

7   **Presentation**   48

8   **Punctuation matters**   54

9   **Make sentences make sense**   64

10   **Making sources work**   74

11   **Referencing**   82

Conclusion   90

introduction

Writing is important. The ability to communicate clearly and effectively is one of the most useful skills you can learn. Whatever you study at school, college or university, and whatever career you choose, a command of language is a valuable asset. Learning to write well can add some extra polish and a few extra marks to your coursework; it can also help to sharpen the way that you think. Good language skills are vital in the workplace, where many different kinds of jobs require the ability to write reports, letters or marketing copy, or to give talks or presentations.

This book will show you how to write well. It focuses on writing essays and dissertations as part of assessed work at college or university, and will also be helpful for projects in the final stages of study at school. This book explains what markers are looking for in written work, and how to achieve this. Tutors often reserve around 20 per cent of an essay mark for issues of presentation and expression, so improving in these areas can make a dramatic difference to your results. Good language skills will also help you create stronger arguments and present your ideas in the best light. Writing well is vital for success at all levels of study. Good writing is also important in many different areas of life, so the advice in this book will be of benefit to others with a wide range of jobs and interests.

Many people are daunted by concepts such as grammar, essay structure or referencing, especially if they prefer working in a subject with a strong practical or scientific element. If this applies to you, do not worry. Good writing isn't rocket science – not even if you are studying rocket science. Most common language problems are easy to fix, and the underlying principles of good writing are simple. Having said that, the process of learning to write well is never complete; there is always something else to correct or to try out. So, even if you are a confident writer, I hope that this book will give you things to think about and will help you to develop your own style and voice.

Every piece of writing, whether an academic essay, a newspaper article, a medical report or a book about writing essays, has a particular job to do, in a particular context, for a particular kind of reader. One of the hardest things about academic writing is working out exactly what sort of format you are supposed to follow and what tone of voice you are supposed to use. This can vary from subject to subject, sometimes even from project to project. However, the basic rules of good writing are the same across the board. You will produce good work when you:

1 understand what sort of piece you are writing and who will read it
2 plan your structure carefully, so that your argument runs clearly
3 use language correctly and efficiently
4 use your sources effectively and reference them properly.

One of the simplest ways to improve your writing is to read a wide range of different kinds of texts – from novels and newspapers to Nobel Prize-winning essays. Try to develop an eye for the different styles and structures these texts use. As you improve your language skills, you will also sharpen your understanding of your own subject. Good reading and writing skills are not an optional extra to your studies; they are right at the core of the education system. Make these a priority and you will quickly become a more perceptive reader. Soon you will also be able to express your own ideas with force and clarity. I cannot promise that all your writing problems will disappear overnight, but I can assure you that once you start paying more attention to this element of your work, you will begin to find the feedback you receive more useful, and you will pick up new skills in handling language and forming arguments. After that, it is up to you to make sure you have something interesting to say.

1

before you begin

Why write essays at all? Many people have never stopped to think about what an essay is or what it does. This chapter will help you to see that an essay is more than a test of your knowledge of a subject. Writing an essay can also be an opportunity to develop key intellectual skills, such as researching, applying a methodology, forming an argument, using sources, and presenting your work clearly and accurately. When your marker comes to read your essay, they will not only get a picture of what you know, but also how you found out about it, and how well you understand it. This chapter will help you to look at your written work in the context of a wider programme of learning, and to think about what your marker will be hoping to see.

There are many different kinds of essay. A mid-term assessment is likely to be a piece of written work of around 1,500 to 3,000 words, focusing on a specific area of your course. Chapter 2 looks at some of the different kinds of essays you might be asked to write. At some point in your studies you will probably have to sit exams, which may involve short essays of a few pages, planned and executed in a high-pressure situation. Your programme of study may also include a dissertation – a long piece of work on a larger project, researched and written over a period of weeks or months. Later in this book, I will have some specific things to say about exams and dissertations, but mostly I will use the term 'essay' to cover all of these, as the basic rules apply to all of them. If you carry on to do postgraduate research or aim for a career in a college or university, the essay-length article will be the most common form that you use to publish your results in academic journals. Conference papers, book reviews and chapters in theses or scholarly books follow very much the same form. Your tutor is probably at work on one of these right now, and may be finding it as troublesome as you found your last essay – which is always a comforting thought.

Although it may not seem obvious to you, your essay has been set as an integral part of your course or degree programme. Committees have deliberated about its length and form, and the questions are likely to have been approved by several members of staff, possibly even by experts from another university. Your essay is a vital component in your course of study, not a random IQ test. It can be very helpful to stop and think for a few minutes about why your tutors have set an essay, rather than a different kind of assessment, and about which elements they are testing.

In modern academic life, issues about core skills and content in courses are quite closely regulated, which is why at the beginning of every term you will be given a course handbook or referred to a web page explaining what your course is about. These do not often make riveting reading. However, they can be a valuable source of inside information about what markers want to see in written work. Try to find the section that is about 'learning outcomes' or 'aims and objectives'. This offers a kind of X-ray view of your course. It allows you to see under the surface and get a picture of what your tutors and lecturers consider the essential framework.

In the description of the course there is usually a section about 'knowledge' or 'content', which focuses on the kind of material you should have learned over the term. For example: an understanding of the place of class and gender in nineteenth-century culture, or the effect of carbon dioxide levels on tree growth, or the usefulness of object teaching in primary schools. There is also usually a section about 'skills' or 'outcomes', which focuses on things your tutors want you to be able to do. For example: evaluate a range of historical sources and secondary reading, or gather and analyse data effectively, or collate and evaluate a series of case studies. One of the things your essay should do is show that you have successfully engaged with the course. So, try to keep these aims and outcomes in mind as you write, and let your marker see that you have been developing skills and knowledge in the relevant areas.

Your course guide can also give you a good idea of what you will need to do to plan a successful piece of written work. If you are expected to evaluate a range of historical sources and secondary reading, you will obviously need to factor in a lot of time in the library. If you are gathering and analysing data, you may need to spend less time in the book stacks, but more time thinking out a questionnaire for a survey, finding candidates to interview, adding up the results and designing graphs and charts. Some of these skills will be specific to your discipline. This book will not be able to help you much with these. You are much better getting expert advice from your lecturers and tutors on the technicalities of your subject. However, there are some activities that are much the same whatever you are studying.

Every piece of written work requires:
* **planning:** choosing a topic and deciding how to approach it
* **research:** gathering the right kind of material
* **thought:** analysing this material and forming a conclusion
* **more planning:** deciding how to present your ideas and results

* **writing:** putting it into words
* **editing:** rereading to correct mistakes and improve presentation.

These are essential for almost any project, but it is remarkable how many students think they can get by just on research and writing. Most essays and dissertations show evidence of some thought, in varying quantities, but planning and editing are often squeezed out because they take a lot of extra time. There is always some smart cookie in a class who can start on a piece of work two days before the deadline and get a decent result. However, these essays hardly ever get the highest marks. Even when written with flair and style, they are usually poorly organized, full of surface errors, and could have been a lot better given a bit more effort. First-class work is always the product of careful thought and attention to detail. Academics often describe high-quality work as 'rigorous', meaning that you can see a probing and hardworking mind at work. This does not mean it is dull – far from it. Often it is the mix of precision and originality that really makes an essay sparkle.

If you are serious about improving your work, you should get going early. If you have a job or family commitments, plan your time very carefully. Try to leave some extra time to allow for something unexpected. Honing your study skills takes years, and to be honest, some highly successful academics never quite learn to organize their time efficiently or meet all their deadlines. But on the whole it will help your written work if you are organized, approach the task in a methodical manner, get hold of the right resources early on, and leave yourself enough time to actually enjoy the process of learning and writing. After all, you chose your course, and you, or someone near and dear to you, may be paying a good deal of money for the privilege of studying. So, you might as well make the most of it.

Whatever subject you are studying and whatever topic you choose for your assignment, it is likely to be assessed according to the same basic principles. Somewhere on your college or university website, there will be a list of marking criteria, which lets you see the rules by which markers operate. At my own university there are five basic criteria, which apply to every subject. Each piece of written work is judged on:

1 understanding and appreciation of the issue(s) raised by the question or topic
2 knowledge of and skill in using, and where appropriate, analysing particular concepts and/or sources
3 relevance and fullness of the answer
4 use of arguments and/or evidence to support observations and conclusions
5 ability to express ideas and/or arguments clearly, cogently and coherently.

The item on the list that is to do with expression and/or presentation often comes at the bottom of such lists of marking criteria. But remember that when your marker picks up your essay, they will start making a judgement about your abilities in this area before they have finished the first paragraph. Spelling mistakes or weird fonts on the cover sheet do not help either. Just as you would want to tidy up before going on a date or giving a presentation, it is important to make a good first impression with written work. Even a highly intelligent piece of work can get off on the wrong foot if it is poorly presented and does not read well from the start.

Many departments reserve up to 20 per cent of the marking scale for issues of presentation and expression. This is the difference between a first-class mark and a very average second-class. Serious problems with grammar and referencing can obscure your argument so badly that you may fail the assessment altogether. Some departments, especially in science-based subjects, say that they do not penalize poor grammar and spelling 'where the meaning is clear'. But the fact is that a cleanly presented essay with good grammar and spelling is always going to do better than a scruffy, poorly written one with similar content. If you want to pick up some extra marks for your work, this is probably the easiest place to start. Good presentation skills are also highly valued by employers in an age when nobody seems to know where to put apostrophes any more. So any effort in this area will be time well spent.

Markers vary hugely in the amount and quality of feedback which they give. It is not necessarily a bad thing if your essay comes back full of notes in the margin. This probably means that you have a highly engaged marker, who is likely to be exactly the kind of person who can help you develop your writing skills. Even if they have given you a less than brilliant mark, this could be the start of an upward trend in your work. Individual feedback is probably the best tool for improving your writing.

Make sure you read all the feedback you get, not just the summarizing comments. Sometimes the most pithy remarks are the little queries and sarcastic comments in the margin. Try not to take offence if your marker has scored out some of your pet phrases or has altered your sentence structure. The chances are that they are trying to show you how you could make your language cleaner and sharper, or how to use a more appropriate register for academic writing. Pay particular attention if the same comments crop up repeatedly, especially if you are getting the same feedback from more than one marker. In this case, something is definitely wrong. The golden rule of capitalizing on essay feedback is to reread the comments from the previous essay before you start the next one. You will be less likely to make the same mistakes all over again, and you will be able to develop your thinking and writing skills in the right direction.

Alternatively, your essay may come back with very few notes in the margin. This can mean one of several things: your essay may be so good that it does not need much correcting; you may have a marker who cannot be bothered to offer much constructive advice; or you may have a good-natured marker who has come to the conclusion that a lot of students simply do not read comments in the margin. Whatever your marker has put on your paper, you are entitled to discuss your work with them. Some departments have a policy of handing back essays individually, using this as a chance for a one-to-one chat with the student about their work. If you are in one of these departments, count yourself lucky. This practice is becoming rarer and rarer. However, even very large and busy departments have a policy of making staff available to see students to discuss their progress. If you would like more feedback than you are getting, or do not understand what your marker has said, it is worth going to see them.

Staff usually have office hours, once or twice a week, in which they have an 'open door' to students. If you want to see your tutor, try to go during their office hour, or email to arrange a time, rather than just dropping in when it suits you. The worst time to attempt to catch your tutor is at ten to the hour, when they are likely to be on the point of getting ready to teach another class. If you want to talk about your work in some depth, leave your essay with your tutor and arrange to come back in a day or two. Remember that the last time they saw it, probably a couple of week ago, it was in a pile of other papers on similar topics, so they may want to read it through again before discussing it.

Talking about your work with your tutor is most productive when you have read through the feedback carefully and when you come with some specific questions about how you could do better. Try not to ask, 'Why did I only get a third-class mark?'. You will get a more helpful answer if you ask, 'How should I have structured my answer?' or 'Did I use the right kind of sources?'. Do not attempt to convince your tutor that your way of doing things was right after all. Try to find out exactly where things went wrong and what you should do next time to put them right. If you really want to improve your work, ask if there is a member of staff or a study skills unit on campus who can help with your writing skills. Study skills tutors are often seen as emergency support for struggling students, but they are sometimes willing to help mid-stream students who believe they can do better. If you have medical or emotional problems that may interfere with your work, make sure you tell your tutor. Most colleges and universities can offer support.

2

know your assignment

Not all essays are the same. Different disciplines need to test different kinds of abilities and have developed a wide variety of projects and assignments to focus on these. If you are doing a joint degree, or if you are studying at a university or college where you have the opportunity to select courses from a variety of subjects, you have probably noticed already that different departments expect slightly different things from you. Even if you are working within one area of study, you are likely to be asked to complete several different kinds of assignment throughout your programme of study. Exams call for specialized skills, and longer pieces of work such as dissertations have their own challenges too. This chapter will help you think about what sort of essay you are writing, and which areas of your knowledge and skill it will test.

Formal essay

The formal essay is the type of assessment most commonly set in colleges and universities, especially in the areas of arts, humanities, social sciences and education. However, you may also have to write formal essays for courses in sciences and medicine. The term 'essay' was invented by the French writer Montaigne in 1580 for his collection of *Essais*. In French the word means 'attempts' and it can be useful to think of your essay as an opportunity to 'try out' an idea or theory. The term was first used in English by Francis Bacon in the late sixteenth century and has been around ever since. It is usually used to describe a balanced, methodical, but not exhaustive, discussion of a single issue or question in a short written form. There is also an 'informal' essay form, in which the writer discusses a subject in a relaxed, personal, light-hearted way, much like a newspaper column. Try to remember that an academic essay is of the formal variety. No wisecracks, please.

Formal essays can vary in length, but at undergraduate level they are most likely to be between 1,500 and 3,000 words. The standard structure of the formal essay has its roots in Classical rhetoric in which a speaker offered a speech in five parts:

1 **introduction:** outlining the topic in hand
2 **statement:** presenting one side of the argument
3 **counterstatement:** presenting the other side of the argument
4 **analysis:** weighing up which side is best
5 **conclusion:** stating the outcome.

The job of the formal essay is to offer a measured discussion on a subject which is in some way open to debate or interpretation, and to draw a reasonable conclusion. It is designed to test your knowledge of the subject, your ability to gather and evaluate evidence, your powers of logical analysis, and your handling of language. It is an all-round intellectual workout.

Literature review

Some essay forms are designed to develop specific skills. The literature review is used in a variety of disciplines to teach students how to engage with the published scholarship on a particular subject. This assignment usually involves summarizing a number of publications and discussing how these support or contradict one another. You may be asked to compare two texts, or you may be asked to present a spectrum of views from a variety of scholars and sources. In this case it can help to think of the review as a round-table discussion on the subject, with yourself in charge. Which experts should you invite to create a lively and probing debate?

For example, your review might include:
* a seminal text establishing the boundaries of the discipline
* a recent text on your topic by an eminent scholar in the field
* a review criticizing or praising the newer text
* a journal article exploring the topic from a different perspective
* a theorized discussion of the terminology used in the discipline
* an online journal article outlining a new project which promises to complete more research in the area, thus moving the debate forward.

You do not have to agree with all the texts you discuss, but make sure that every text you cite connects tightly to the subject at the core of the assignment. Remember, the review is designed to teach you how to find, digest and evaluate scholarly literature in your field, and to introduce you to a range of views on the subject you are studying.

Project report

If you are studying a subject with an element of practical research, you will be asked to write project reports. These are essential for lab work, fieldwork and survey work in a variety of subjects from microbiology to psychology. Most scientific journal articles are structured in the form of the project report, so mastering this kind of assignment is a key skill for many students. The project report should explain what your project was about, how you went about it and what your results were. If you are working as part of a team, it should make clear exactly what your role was within the project.

A project report begins with a short abstract of 100–200 words. This should give a brief indication of the aim of the project, the methods used and the outcome. After the abstract, your introduction should explain the aims of the project and the methods and materials used. You might want to include some secondary literature at this stage to explain your use of one particular method. The main section of the report will describe the research or experiments you carried out and the results. You may want to use graphs and diagrams to display your results. Make sure these are clearly and correctly labelled, but do not leave them to speak entirely for themselves. Summarize what they show and explain the significance of this. You will then need to discuss and analyse your results, referring to other research in the area if appropriate. Lastly, state your conclusion.

The purpose of the project report is not simply to show that you and your project team arrived at the 'right answer' during your research. The report should show:

* that you carried out your project using appropriate methods
* that you applied these carefully
* that you kept careful records
* that you analysed your data sensibly
* that you took account of relevant scholarship
* that you were aware of other methods or approaches that could have been used.

These are all key skills in academic research. Let your marker see that you are developing these abilities.

Learning log

A learning log, as its name suggests, is a record or diary of your learning. You are most likely to be asked to keep a learning log in subjects such as teaching, nursing or social work, where you are learning skills of professional practice. It is also beginning to appear as a course requirement in other academic subjects, but anybody can keep a learning log. This can be a good way to improve your study skills and make you a more effective learner.

The key skill for a learning log is self-evaluation, also called reflective practice or critical reflection. Many careers require regular self-evaluation, so this is a good skill to learn now. Your learning log is not just a record of what you did or the knowledge you acquired; it is an opportunity to reflect on your learning experience, how you felt about it, and how you can develop skills in the future. You may find it helpful to have a checklist of questions which you work through at each entry so that you can see how you are progressing in each area. These questions might include:

* What did I do?
* What theory did I put into practice?
* What ideas did it throw up?
* How did it make me feel?
* How well/badly did it go?
* What did I learn about my subject?
* What did I learn about myself?
* What skills do I need to develop?
* What will I do differently next time?
* How have I progressed since last time?

Be honest about the areas where you need to improve, but focus on your strengths and develop strategies for using them.

Case study

Case studies are used in many different disciplines to explore the impact of a situation or a methodological approach on a particular person or group. You may be asked to write a case study based on a practical project in which you have been involved, or you may be asked to research a documented event through source material. In some exercises you could be asked to compare two similar cases. The hallmark of a case study is that you are writing about a genuine situation involving real people.

As with a project report, it is important to offer a balance of information and analysis in a case study. Make sure you are thoroughly familiar with the facts of your case and with the theoretical method that you plan to use to analyse it. Try to think critically about both these elements. Do you have all the information you need? Is your method appropriate for this particular case? You should give a summary of the narrative of the case in the introduction. However, in the main body of the text do not devote all your energy and word count to describing what happened. Remember that your task is to analyse the situation. You should:

* demonstrate your knowledge of the case
* look for the causes of events
* relate what happened to relevant theories in your discipline
* assess the effects of any actions or developments
* show what can be learned from this particular case
* propose solutions or further research.

Close reading

Close reading is a standard form of assessment in subjects which depend upon a lot of textual sources, such as literature, history and religious studies. In this kind of exercise you are given a short piece of text, which you are expected to analyse both for content and for style of expression. This exercise can also be called critical analysis, textual analysis, practical criticism, exegesis, or a gobbet question. In case you were wondering, a 'gobbet' is an Old English word that refers to a tasty morsel plucked out of a pot of stew. This word is often used by historians to refer to a particularly interesting section of an historical document which is worth chewing over – which is actually quite a good way to think about this kind of project.

Avoid speculating about things that are not in the text, or guessing who wrote it, unless you know for sure. Tie everything you say back to specific things in the passage. Make sure you do not just discuss what the passage says. Look at how this is expressed. Ask yourself these questions:

* What does this text reveal about its own origins and context?
* What sort of reader does it imply or assume?
* What ideas or questions does it raise?
* How does it make me feel?
* Which words or phrases seem most important or effective?
* Does it use a particular style of expression, for example, formal, legal, conversational, biblical or poetic?
* Are there any recurring patterns or strategies within the passage?
* Is the language concrete and particular or abstract and general?

Learning to be a shrewd, critical reader is also one of the best ways of sharpening up your own writing. As you begin to recognize the strategies which other writers use, you can learn about your own style and about how to make language work more effectively.

Exam

The formal essay is the most common type of essay question in an exam setting. However, you should never assume that this is what you will get. Check your course guide and talk to your tutor. You should be given clear advice before the exam on the kind of questions that will come up, but sometimes you do have to ask.

When you are revising for the exam think carefully about the types of skills your marker wants you to demonstrate in your answer. This can be a good time to go back and look at the course aims or learning outcomes in the course guide. Try to focus your answer towards these aims and outcomes. In the exam you will have to make decisions quickly. Knowing the course aims and outcomes can help you to choose which bits of information to use and how to present them.

Make sure you take a few minutes to make a plan for your answer. As a marker of many exam scripts, I can tell you that the best answers usually have a plan on the first page of the exam booklet. Put a line through any planning material in your script, so that your marker knows this page should not be marked. A plan will help to keep you on track as you write. It also gives you somewhere to jot down notes of relevant material you want to use. Under exam pressure it can be easy to forget something that seemed crystal clear 15 minutes ago. So, make a quick note when you think of something.

Look at old exam papers for your course to get an idea of the kinds of questions that will come up. This is always helpful. Make sure you also have a good look at the 'rubric'. This is the set of instructions at the front or top of the exam paper. These can give some valuable clues about what your marker wants to see. You should also read this carefully on the day of your own exam as it may be slightly different from last year's paper.

If you are sitting an 'open book' exam, in which you are allowed to bring in certain set texts, make sure you use them. Allowing you to have these texts in the exam hall is a sure sign that you are expected to know your way around them and to quote from them. Demonstrate your ability to do this. Give clear references and page numbers.

Similarly, if you are allowed to bring in protractors, rulers and coloured pencils, this probably means that you are expected to be able to present some of your material in graph or diagram form. Be prepared for this, and always check your numbers carefully. It is easy to slip up under pressure. As in essays, connect your visual material to your text. You should explain and analyse the information contained in your graphs and diagrams.

Markers are usually fairly tolerant about minor errors and slips of the pen in exams, so long as your meaning is clear. However, you can do yourself a big favour by handing in a paper that is neat, readable and written with style and accuracy. If you usually type lecture notes and essays, give yourself some practice writing longhand, and make sure your handwriting is legible. It may make sense to you, but can anybody else decipher it? Always think about who might read your work and make life easy for them.

Finally, bring a spare pen. It is amazing how many people forget.

Dissertation

Writing a dissertation can seem a daunting task. This is likely to be the longest piece of work you have tackled so far. It is also likely to count for a considerable proportion of your final result. This may be the first time that you have taken on a project on a different topic from any of your classmates. However, there is no need to panic. You are likely to have the expert help of a supervisor who has seen many similar projects safely to conclusion. You are also likely to be nearing the end of your programme of study. Even if you do not feel like it, you probably already have most of the abilities that you need to complete a successful dissertation. If you have been paying anything like attention over the past few months and years, you will have been quietly building up the skills and knowledge that you need for this project.

The length and form of your dissertation will depend upon the type of subject you are studying. However, it is likely to develop the essay skills that you have already learned during your studies. If most of your written work so far has been of the formal essay type, it is likely that your dissertation will be an extended version of this form. Some humanities subjects call the dissertation a 'long essay', which suggests just this. If your coursework has included a mix of assessments, (for example, literature reviews, project reports and formal essays), then it is likely that your dissertation should include elements of all of these. Discuss the form of your dissertation carefully with your supervisor before you start doing your research. You will need to know what kind of material you need before you plan your project.

Organize your time before you start by writing a timetable for the project. Work back from the submission date and leave yourself plenty of extra time, especially in the final stages. Break the project up into workable sections and set yourself achievable targets for each stage. Work out what you need to organize in terms of practical elements, such as lab work, surveys or fieldwork. Try to get a lot of the reading done early, especially if your project includes a literature review section. This will sharpen up your own thinking on your topic and will give you some good ideas for organizing and presenting your project.

As you are likely to spend weeks, perhaps even months, working on your dissertation, it is important that you choose an area of research that you find interesting and that you feel you can handle confidently. Departments vary in the amount of freedom students are given in choosing topics, but you should work closely with your supervisor in choosing a topic and working out a question or thesis. Unless you are writing a Ph.D., a dissertation does not have to be a groundbreaking piece of research, but it should have some level of originality. So, work creatively with your supervisor to challenge assumptions and to create new perspectives.

Take account of any advice your supervisor gives on choosing a topic. They will have seen many projects come and go, and they are likely to know what is possible with the time and resources available. Many students at dissertation level want to take on very ambitious projects that would be more suited to a Ph.D. project, or even a major international research project with several full-time researchers. If this applies to you, and you feel passionately about the subject, then consider applying to do research in that area – after you have finished your dissertation. At this stage it is better to choose something manageable and execute it well.

A good way to generate a topic is to think about a set of classes or an assessment which you particularly enjoyed and in which you did well. Was there anything in those classes or in that assessment on which you would like to spend more time? Did any of your project, reports or case studies suggest further research in a similar area that you would like to follow up? Could you expand some work that you did earlier to look at a similar issue in more depth or by using a different method? Discuss with your supervisor whether you are allowed to tackle similar material twice. Some departments have strict rules about not writing on the same text, topic or case study more than once. However, it is usually possible to do something similar or in a related area. There is more advice on finding a topic in the next chapter.

If your supervisor says that they are not qualified to supervise the particular project that you want to do, then choose a different topic or ask for a different supervisor. Do not forge ahead regardless. There are no medals for bravery in dissertations. Keep in touch with your supervisor throughout the project, and take their advice seriously. However brilliant your ideas may be, the fact is that your supervisor has more experience than you, and is likely to be able to help you save time and avoid simple errors. They will also be able to keep you straight on issues of presentation and referencing, which are often marked more strictly at dissertation level. So heed any advice given in this area.

3

questions and topics

The easiest way to fail an assessment is not to answer the question. So, it is important that you understand how your question works and what you are expected to do with it. For many assignments, you will be given an element of choice about your subject. Either you will be asked to select a question from a list, or you will be invited to suggest a topic of your own. Choosing the right subject for your essay or dissertation can be vital to success. But what is the right subject? How can you tell which topic is going to allow you to produce your best work? How can you be sure that you understand the question? This chapter will give you advice on these issues, and will give you some hints about how to read the language used in essay questions.

You might think that choosing a question is the first stage of your assignment. Some students pick a question from the course guide before the course has even started. However, you are probably wiser to wait and do a bit of thinking and research before you finalize your essay topic. When you read through the list of essay questions provided for your course or suggested dissertation topics, there will probably be one that jumps out at you as the most obvious or the easiest to answer. This may not be the smart one to choose. An easy question often leads to a very average answer, while something a little more challenging may allow you to produce a really top-flight piece of work. The obvious choice may also be very popular with your classmates, so you might find yourself competing with a number of other students for the relevant resources in the library.

It can be hard to tell which question will help you to create a good essay, but generally a focused question gives you a better chance of writing a strong, focused answer. As a rough rule of thumb, focused questions make it clear how you should approach your research and frame your answer. Broad questions are open, can be interpreted in different ways and offer little direction. For example, the following looks like an easy question on an interesting topic:

Consider the connection between marriage and money in the nineteenth century.

However, this question is almost impossible to answer well. It is very loose and does not give you a clear idea of where you should direct your energies. It is not even clear which discipline it belongs to: literature, gender studies, cultural history, sociology, or something else. 'Consider' is also a rather vague verb. It suggests that you should have a think about the topic, but it does not make it clear how you should structure your answer. What is more, the nineteenth century is a very long time. There is no chance of being able to deal with all of it in a short piece of coursework. This question gives you very little idea where to start.

On the other hand, the following looks like a harder question on a similar subject:

Assess the impact of the 1882 Married Women's Property Act on the lives of Victorian women.

In reality, this is much easier to answer well. You are being asked to display your knowledge and understanding of the causes and effects of one particular event. You are being invited to do some reading and research on what life was like for Victorian women (but not for men or children) before and after the 1882 Act. You are still being left a fair amount of freedom about which women you want to write about and how you will structure your essay. For example, you could focus on middle-class women, or compare the lives of upper-class and working-class women. However, from the use of the phrase 'assess the impact', it is absolutely clear that your essay should form a judgement about the importance or otherwise of the 1882 Act. By looking carefully at the question you are already well on your way to planning your answer.

Some essay questions are phrased as questions; they ask what, how, where, when and why, and have a question mark at the end. For example:

Are the UN's weaknesses also its greatest assets?

What is the relevance of the artist's intention to interpreting works of art?

What does it mean to say violence is gendered?

How has the notion of the body operated in anthropology in recent years?

Such questions are usually strong, focused questions with a clear aim built into them. However, they still require some analysis and may have weaknesses. Think about each of the words in the question. They are probably all important and should direct you towards what you are expected to do.

Alternatively, many questions are phrased as instructions. These can be more tricky. For example:

Discuss Ishmael's role as narrator in **Moby Dick.**

Evaluate the importance of handcrafts in modern-day Inuit culture.

Analyse the effect of building society interest rates on London property prices since 2000.

Compare US President Woodrow Wilson's attitude to American national identity to that of President Theodore Roosevelt.

Many students pay attention to the subject of the essay, but gloss over the instructions about what they are being asked to do. Make sure you read the verbs in the questions as well as the nouns. The verbs tell you what action is required. Many of these verbs belong to an academic vocabulary that can seem a little confusing, but they fall into several general groups.

Discuss, Explore, Consider, Examine: These words are all likely to be used in a formal essay question to invite a thorough discussion about the topic. In this kind of question there is often some room for creativity about how you approach your subject or what you choose to focus on. However, do not be fooled into thinking that you can just raise a few issues involved in the topic and then leave it there. You still need to include evidence and analysis, and to draw a strong conclusion to make this work.

Analyse, Evaluate, Assess, Demonstrate, Criticize: These terms all require a rigorous, systematic approach to your topic or project. You are being asked to show your understanding of certain processes and to form judgements about the quality of the evidence in the area of your topic. For this kind of question you need a tightly argued structure, and you may also be wise to use a methodological approach to show that you can handle your material logically and with accuracy.

Differentiate, Distinguish, Compare, Contrast, Relate: These words are used in questions where you are being asked to navigate between two topics or statements. You will need to discuss both the connections and differences between the two and look at the causes and implications of these connections and differences. Do not be tempted to write a short essay on one topic followed by a short essay on the other. Keep a dialogue between the two alive throughout the essay. This will create a much stronger answer to the question.

Describe, Review, State, Summarize: These terms call for an essay rich in information, but lighter on analysis. You may be asked to recount how you went about an experiment, to give an overview of the main points of a topic or argument, or to review recent literature in your field. This kind of question is testing your skills of selection and summary.

Prove, Justify, Defend: Provide evidence and argument to support a statement or conclusion.

Disprove, Refute: Provide evidence and argument to contradict a statement or conclusion.

Choosing your own topic

Choosing your own topic is much easier if you understand how to choose and read set questions. So, if you have skipped the previous sections in this chapter, go back and read them before going on. Pay special attention to the difference between broad and focused questions. If you are invited to choose your own topic for a project, essay or dissertation, you want to set yourself a strong question. This will make it easier for you to write a strong answer. It also helps your marker to see what your main aims are. Try to construct a sharp, focused question that gives your work direction and provides some structure for your answer.

Remember to build on what you have been learning in class and show off your new skills and knowledge. As with choosing a set question, this can be a good time to plan a session in the library to see what resources are available and what catches your interest.

4

finding the right material

Choosing and using sources is an integral part of studying. Finding useful texts can seem difficult, especially if most of the texts recommended in your course guide have been checked out of the library before you get there. Your tutor will not be impressed if you give up searching, and write a superficial essay or dissertation built up of information from lecture notes and study-notes sites on the internet. However, there is no need to panic. There are thousands of books in your college or university library, and a whole range of up-to-date and reliable electronic sources which you can explore. Dozens of these will be relevant to your topic. The trick is knowing where to look. This chapter will give you some advice on how to develop your research skills, and find sources which will inform your work and give you interesting ideas.

Academic journals

Academic journals are a key resource for students in most science and social-science subjects. Journals present peer-reviewed research. This means that the research in each of these journals has been read and evaluated by other experts in the same field. They are often published by university presses. You can therefore assume that this research has been thoroughly critiqued and checked by capable scholars. Journal articles offer up-to-date, reliable research.

The easiest way to find relevant information in your field is to go to an online search engine such as Ingenta, Intute, JSTOR, LION, Project MUSE or PubMed. Ask your tutor which one is the most appropriate for your subject. Or try looking on your department or library web page. These often provide useful links to the best search engines. Look under 'study resources' or 'subject resources'. Most search engines allow you to search by key words, so that you can find material relevant to your project. You will be able to access some journals online, but for others you will have to actually go to the library and check out the journal. Some disciplines have one or two key journals that dominate debate. For example, in medicine, *The Lancet* and the *BMJ* have very strong reputations and are likely to get the pick of the best research. Find out which journals are most important for your discipline and keep an eye out for anything interesting there.

Books

Many students are so reliant on online sources that they forget about the wealth of printed material in the library. In some science subjects you will not be encouraged to rely on book material, but for many academic disciplines the book is still seen as the most authoritative source for research. Your course guide may suggest some key texts for you to look at, but you need not stop at the end of this list. Aim to get a sense of what is in your library, and try out lots of different combinations of key words on your library computer to see what comes up.

The trouble with computer catalogues is that they often encourage you to look for one book at a time, find it and check it out, without stopping to browse. Books are usually shelved by subject, so the books nearby are likely to be dealing with similar topics. It can be tremendously useful to spend a few minutes looking along the book stacks to see if there is anything else relevant. Read the blurb on the cover, check the contents page and have a quick look at the introduction. These should give you a good idea if it might be useful or not. If you do find a particularly useful book, it is often worth looking in the bibliography at the back for ideas of more things to read. Your library probably has some of these books too.

Internet sources

There are many interesting and scholarly pieces of work on the internet. There is also a lot of superficial and inaccurate information. Be very careful about what you use from the internet. Sites which are sponsored by universities, academic publishers, academic societies or government departments are likely to give you very good information. Check the source of your information by looking at the second section of the url address. Think carefully before using and citing a source that includes **.com** or **.co.uk.** Unless you know this is a reliable source, choose something else. The following addresses are more likely to be dependable:

.ac.uk – a UK university, college or school

.edu – a US university, college or school

.org – a professional organization or society

.gov – a government or civil service department

Look on your department website for a list of useful and reliable links in your field.

Be especially wary of study-notes sites, which may not bring your work up to the level that your tutors would like to see. Also, discussion boards and essays that are not published through a recognizable academic site often contain information which is simply not correct. There is nothing to stop you posting your work on the internet, so what you find through Google could just be the work of an enthusiastic undergraduate with some computing skills. Your marker will get twitchy if most of your bibliography is made up of internet sites. Make sure you use a mix of sources as you do your research. Reference internet material as carefully as you would reference printed material. Chapter 11 will show you how.

Effective reading is a complex skill and requires a lot of practice. As you explore your sources, think about how you can get the most out of them. Before you start on a text, think about the sort of things you are looking for to help your project along, but do not be so blinkered that you ignore other interesting elements when they crop up. Everyone has their own way of approaching a text, and for different assignments you will be looking for different things. However, here are a few strategies for reading:

* **Keep an open mind about the text.** One of the most valuable things you can learn as you study is the ability to suspend your own prejudices and preconceptions as you read. Learning to see things from different perspectives is a vital part of the reading process. Do not attempt to make a text fit your own agenda as you go along, or dismiss it because it challenges what you believe. You do not have to agree with the text, but give it a chance to speak for itself. If you react strongly to something, try to work out why.

* **Be critical.** This sounds like a contradiction of the previous point, but it is not. Critical thinking is more about asking questions than forming judgements. So, as you read, ask yourself questions about the text. These will help you decide whether the text is sound or not. Ask the kind of questions a marker might ask about an essay. How accurate is it? Has the author missed something important? Have they used a useful method or approach? Did they apply it carefully? Have they come to a reasonable conclusion? Does the author seem to have a particular underlying agenda that may be clouding their judgement? Remember that a flawed text can be very useful when you are constructing an essay. So, if you find something you disagree with, do not put the text back on the bookshelf. You can use it in your essay and argue against it.

* **Think about language.** Keep one eye open for the language the author uses. This is especially important if you are studying literary texts. However, it is a useful way to read academic books and journals too. Language does more than tell a story. It creates a world of ideas. So, do not just look at what the text says. Think about how it communicates with the reader. Doing this will sharpen up your writing too.

5

planning
and
structure

Markers sometimes complain about poor structure in an essay as though this was a problem of presentation. However, if your essay has gone wrong in this area, it is probably because of something that happened, or didn't happen, long before you actually started writing. Bad structure in an essay is usually the result of a failure to read the question carefully, a lack of understanding of the subject, or a rushed job. Take time to plan your work. This ensures that you connect your essay with the question. It reduces the stress of writing, as you know where you are going next. It produces a well-rounded piece of writing and a satisfying read for your marker. This chapter will give you some advice on how to construct a plan that fits your assignment, and how to use paragraphs to make the shape of your essay clear.

Whatever way you like to take notes and marshal your ideas, at some point you are going to need a linear plan for your essay. It is always worth doing this, especially in exams when time is tight and nerves are likely to make you forget a good idea or a useful piece of evidence. Remember what kind of essay you are writing. This is a good point to flick back to Chapter 2 and remind yourself of the shape of your assignment.

If you are writing a formal essay, you probably want to think about how your material fits the form of an introduction, a statement, a counterstatement, an analysis and a conclusion. If you are writing a project report, you will want to construct a plan that follows the model of abstract, aims of the project, methods used, results, discussion, conclusion. In some essays the plan is not quite so rigid. For example, a close reading can work through the set passage from beginning to end, or your question may ask you to look at certain themes or elements. In this case you should probably construct a plan with an introduction, a section for each theme and a conclusion. A case study could follow a formal essay pattern, or could work more like a project report. Be guided by your question and by the conventions of your subject. If you are in doubt, check with your tutor. Ask them to spend some time during a tutorial on this. The most important thing is to remember that you are not just making lists of what you know or what you have done. You are answering a question and the whole thing should form a logical argument with a clear outcome.

A plan should operate as a skeleton for your essay. Ideally it should be possible for a reader to reconstruct your plan from the finished article. This is often what you are doing when you take lecture notes. Paying attention to how this process works will make planning your own written work a lot easier. Most lecturers think carefully about how they want to present material to the class. It might seem random, but if you listen they will give you markers about what the main headings are, and when they are filling out these sections. Look over your lecture notes and think about some of the techniques lecturers use. Try to see the shape of the lecture:

* Is the lecturer moving outward from a single text or problem to a wider context?
* Are they focusing in, beginning with background information, looking at a large cultural issue or scientific problem, and then exploring how one text or set of results contributes to this debate?
* Are they working through a text or an historical period in order?
* Are they offering a spectrum of different views on one issue?

These are all approaches you can use in structuring your written work. A clear plan makes it easier to fulfil your intentions.

Once you have an outline plan, you can start writing. This can be the hardest moment of the whole essay-writing process. Everyone knows how intimidating a blank screen or page can be, but try not to freeze up at this point. Think of your plan as a map that will keep you on the right route as you navigate your way through your material. However, as with following a map, there is a point where you have to stop thinking about the journey, get your boots on and set off across country. Things often look rather different on the ground from how they look on the map, but that may not be a bad thing. Hopefully, your plan will have helped you to divide your material into several workable sections, which makes the task more manageable. The challenge at this stage is to put your material together in such a way as to form a coherent argument.

Remember that an argument is more than a disagreement between two or more points of view. The argument of your essay is the line of reasoning which you use to make your point or explain your position. You are doing more than simply setting out facts and data. You are also giving reasons, explaining causes, and drawing conclusions from these. You are showing why the evidence you have chosen supports your conclusion, and you are attempting to persuade the reader to your point of view.

When you drew up the plan for your essay, you probably marked out several sections with subheadings. However, think twice before you type these into your essay in bold script. Some disciplines are very keen on subheadings and subsections within written work. Project reports in science subjects are likely to require subsections which are clearly titled. You may also be required to number your paragraphs, 1.1, 1.2 and so on. This ensures that your report is laid out clearly, that everything is in the correct section, and that your marker can find their way around swiftly. However, in arts and social-science subjects, this may not be required. In fact, it may be seen as fussy and restrictive. A formal essay is the least likely piece of writing to require subheadings or numbered sections, as the point of this exercise is to create a continuous, coherent argument. Breaking a short essay up into subtitled sections can distract from the flow of your essay. Make sure you know what the standard practice is for your subject. If in doubt, check with your tutor.

Think about the plan that you have written for your essay. Think about the sections into which you have divided your argument. If you are writing a short piece of work, it may be appropriate to write a paragraph for each section. However, if you are writing a substantial essay or a dissertation you will probably have to subdivide each section into several paragraphs. Under your section headings you probably have a list of things you want to discuss or evidence you want to use. Allocate a paragraph to each one or, if you have a very complex idea in there, allocate a paragraph to each element of it. When your marker reads your work, they should, ideally, be able to recreate the structure of your essay plan from your paragraphs. Each paragraph should be a step forward in your argument. It should deal with one element of your essay or dissertation thoroughly and efficiently. It can help to think of each paragraph as a mini essay in which you introduce a new idea, present some evidence to back it up, and draw a conclusion from it. Once you have done this, start another one.

Markers are usually suspicious of paragraphs consisting of less than three sentences or rambling on for more than a page. Read through your essay once you have finished. If you find any paragraphs that are too long or too short, consider revising where the breaks fall. Do not use novels or newspapers as models for paragraphing. Novelists and journalists are not writing academic prose and are aiming for very different effects. Journalists rarely have more than one sentence in a paragraph, and often do not write complete sentences. They are playing a different game altogether, so you should not copy what they do. Here again, journal articles or academic books will offer good examples. So, pay attention to this as you do your research and learn to follow the standard practice for your own discipline.

6

introductions and conclusions

Introductions and conclusions can be difficult to write well, but they are not optional extras to your essay or dissertation. These are important sections, which are integral to your argument. Have one of each in every piece of work. The introduction and the conclusion should frame your work, making it clear and accessible to your reader. So, it is important to get these sections right. However, many writers, even at very advanced levels, find constructing introductions and conclusions a challenge. So much seems to hang on these sections that they can appear very daunting. But do not worry. There are some strategies that you can learn which should help. This chapter will give you some ideas and advice about how to create powerful, concise and interesting sections which highlight the main themes and outcomes of your work.

An introduction should make it clear what the essay or dissertation is going to do. It should not be too loose. Do not use your introduction as a general dumping ground for background information that does not seem to fit anywhere else. Nor should you try to approach your topic in a wonderfully inventive, roundabout manner by spending three paragraphs talking about something else which is distantly but cleverly connected to your main idea. Try to zero in quickly on the area of your essay and to announce its main themes and methods.

On the other hand, your introduction should not be too narrow. Avoid repeating or rephrasing your question in the introduction. This gives the impression that in your reading and research you have not developed your ideas in any particular direction. It suggests that the essay which follows will be a rather mechanical, juiceless response to the question, rather than a lively, innovative, independent piece of writing. However, the introduction can be a good place to discuss the themes and problems raised by the question, or to focus in on the particular aspects of the issue which you plan to address.

Some introductions give the impression that the student is scared of the question and does not know what to do with it. Other introductions show that the student is in control of the subject and has an idea of how to tackle it. Try to create an active introduction that gives a sense of what you will do next. Imagine you are answering this question: **Explore the connection between marriage and money in Jane Austen's *Pride and Prejudice*.** A passive introduction would be something like this:

> *Marriage and money are important themes in* Pride and Prejudice. *This essay explores the connection between marriage and money in Jane Austen's novel. First I will look at the theme of marriage, followed by the theme of money. Then I will look at the connection between the two. From this we will be able to see what Austen is trying to say about the link between them.*

There is nothing really wrong with this, but it does not open up the question in an interesting way or provide anything to grab the reader's attention. A good introduction offers a sense of where the essay will go. Something like this is better:

> **The connection between marriage and money lies at the heart of Pride and Prejudice. From the opening sentence to Elizabeth and Darcy's engagement, this novel highlights the desirability of financial security in marriage. However, this novel also shows the dangers of marrying purely for gain. This essay will explore the different models of marriage which Austen presents in Pride and Prejudice: marrying for money without love, marrying for love without money, and marrying with both. These models allow Austen to examine the place of the marriageable woman within the society of her period.**

This introduction demonstrates knowledge of the text and some intelligent thought on the question. It also maps out the plan of the essay that is going to follow.

Conclusions are also hard to handle gracefully, but it is better to try than to ignore the problem. As I have noted before, the easiest way to fail an assignment is to fail to answer the question. The easiest way to fail to answer the question is to avoid writing a conclusion, or to write a conclusion that is so hazy that your final verdict is not obvious. The one thing that a conclusion must do is to conclude. This is your last chance to make the point of your essay crystal clear. Use this opportunity well.

Some students worry that if they give a clear answer to the question they might reach the wrong conclusion and lose marks. However, you are much more likely to lose marks for having no conclusion than for coming to a flawed conclusion. Try to remember that your marker is testing more than your ability to state the correct answer. Your marker is also interested in your ability to use the methods central to your discipline and to argue well. Many essays, especially in arts and social science subjects do not have a 'correct' answer. It may be possible to reach a range of conclusions from the evidence available. What matters is that your essay as a whole builds up a case for the point that you want to make.

Like introductions, conclusions can be weak and purposeless, or they can be active and full of energy. Here is an example of a passive conclusion, which follows on from the passive introduction:

> *In this essay I have looked at the theme of marriage in* **Pride and Prejudice** *and how it connects to the theme of money. From this investigation we can see that Austen has complex views about marriage and money. On the one hand she wants her heroines to marry well and have a secure future, but on the other hand she also believes that people should marry for love. There is a connection between the two because both marriage and money were important for people in Austen's time, which is why they are important themes in* **Pride and Prejudice.**

This conclusion takes account of the fact that there is more than one way of approaching the issue of marriage and money in Austen's novel. However, it fails to offer a judgement about which one is of more significance. Pointing out the complexity of the situation does not offer any closure or resolution, although it could have been a useful way of opening up the issue in the introduction. The final sentence is a mirror image of the opening sentence of the introduction; it also has a strong flavour of the question. The essay in between these two sections may well have been interesting and well informed, but the reader will put the essay down with the impression that this piece of work has not gone anywhere. Now consider this:

> *Austen clearly values love and emotional compatibility as elements of a successful marriage. However, the final pages of* **Pride and Prejudice** *demonstrate that Austen does not believe that a happy marriage is possible without the social and domestic stability which a secure income provides. Her subtle understanding of the part that money plays in sexual*

politics both before and after marriage is one of the hallmarks of her writing. W. H. Auden notes in his poem 'Letter to Lord Byron' (1937) that Jane Austen has a shrewd sense of 'the amorous effects of "brass"'. This unsentimental awareness is, as Auden suggests, the most 'shocking' thing about her.

This conclusion keeps the essay alive and working hard right up to the last full stop.

7

presentation

You can lose the goodwill of your marker before they even start reading your work by presenting an essay or dissertation that is hard to read or poorly presented. Your work will be graded on its content and how well it reads, but this can be helped or hindered by the visual layout of your script and your attention to details of grammar, punctuation and spelling. This chapter will explain some of the quirks of submission regulations for essays, and will help you to think about presentation as an important skill which you can use in many different situations. Learning to edit your own work to weed out errors and to sharpen up your expression is vital too. Show your marker that you care about producing a carefully constructed, neatly presented, error-free text. They will be impressed.

Learning to create a tidy, readable text is a valuable skill in many areas of life and work, so it is worth practising this now. There are several things that you can do to make your script look good. These will not get you extra marks, but they might stop you losing some. They will put your marker in a better frame of mind, which is always a good thing.

* **Whose essay is this?** Make sure that you put your name or student number, your course title and code, and your tutor's name clearly on the cover of your essay. The chances are that you will hand in your essay to a large administrative office where there may be dozens, even hundreds, of pieces of written work from a number of courses being processed at the same time. Make it obvious that this is your work. If your department or school requires you to fill out a cover sheet, make sure that you do this clearly and that it is firmly attached to your script. If you submit your work online or by email, make sure that your name, course title and code are included in the essay document itself, not just in the covering email.

* **Write the question at the top.** It might be obvious to you which question you are answering, but believe me, it is not always clear to the marker. Having the question on your essay also helps you keep the question in mind as you write. So, write the question at the top or on the cover of your essay. However, do not spend hours designing an elaborate title page. Your marker would rather see you put that time and effort into your written work. In exams there is no need to rewrite the question, but mark the number clearly both on your answer and on the front of the paper.

* **Double-space the text.** Many students are reluctant to double-space their text because it costs a few pence more to print out their work. However, your department may require you to double-space your work, and there are several good reasons why you should. First, it makes the text easier to read. Bear in mind that your marker will be reading a lot of essay scripts and will get weary of looking

at words and numbers. Anything you can do to keep your marker awake and happy is likely to work in your favour.

Secondly, if you do not double-space your text, your marker does not have enough space to mark corrections and comments on your work. Remember that essay feedback is a valuable tool for improving your writing. You want to encourage your marker to give as much feedback as possible. Leave space between the lines so that they can.

Finally, double-spacing text is standard practice in most areas of writing and scholarship, so it is a good habit to form. Although newspapers, books and articles are printed by publishers with single-spacing, all of these texts will have started life as double-spaced scripts. I am double-spacing my text as I write this book. This allows copy-editors and proofreaders to spot and correct any errors. If you go on to further study or to a job which involves producing texts of any sort, you will need to double-space your writing. So, start doing this now.

* **Leave a wide margin.** Leave white space on either side of your text. The default settings on your computer will probably give you a margin of 3 cm. This should be adequate, but some departments have strict regulations about the width of margins. If this is the case in your department, then follow the rules that you have been set. The reasons for a margin are the same as for double-spacing. You need to leave room for comments and corrections. These will be useful. Make sure you read them. For a dissertation or thesis that requires binding, leave an extra wide margin of 3.5 cm on the left-hand side of each page. This will ensure that none of your text is lost in the gutter when the typescript is bound.

* **Use a sensible font.** Print your work in Times New Roman or Arial. These are the best fonts as they are easy to read and familiar to the eye. Do not imagine that a curly, cursive font will add class or style to your work. Your tutor will not be impressed. Use 12-point text unless directed otherwise.

Anything smaller is hard to read. Anything bigger suggests that you might be trying to cover up for a short piece of work. Do not put quotations in italics, unless that is how they appear in the text you are quoting. Only use italics for titles of books and plays, or words in a foreign language. You can use bold text for subheadings and subtitles, but not for quotations, book titles or anything that you wish to emphasize in the text.

* **Give clear references.** This is easy when you know how. See Chapter 11.

* **Include a bibliography.** Even if you only have one or two texts to list, you should still provide a bibliography or a reference list on the final page of your script. This is an integral part of your essay and will show your marker that you are recognizing the sources of your material.

* **Include a word count.** Writing to length is a useful skill which you will need later on in life. Learn to tailor your work to the requested word length, and include a word count at the end or on the cover of your essay. If you are having trouble meeting the word limit, read through your essay with a very critical eye. Do you need all those big quotations? Could you cut them down to a phrase or two instead? Is your writing full of little phrases that could be trimmed out, such as: 'it is worthwhile to note that' or 'it seems to be the case that'? Have you given too much detail, or not enough? If your essay is dramatically over or under the limit, you may need to go back and revise your plan for the essay. See the end of this chapter for some more advice about editing your essay.

If your essay is slightly over or under the limit, that is probably fine. Usually, you will not be penalized for an essay that is within 10 per cent of the stated word count, either over or under.

However, you will be penalized for lying about it, so give an accurate word count. When marking essays for a whole class, it is usually easy for the marker to tell when something is too long or too short. Be honest about this or face the consequences.

Editing your work is a vital part of the writing process. When builders finish making a new house, the architect or project manager goes around checking that everything has been done correctly and neatly. When they find things that need tidying up or redoing, they create a 'snagging' list: a wobbly radiator, a door that does not open properly, a cracked piece of skirting board, a leaky tap. A good builder will come back to the house as many times as necessary to get the job just right. A poor builder will say it does not matter, or it is not his job. He has done it once already and is not going to do it all over again. Think of editing your work as finding and fixing these 'snags'. Attention to detail and the willingness to work at getting things right are important and valuable skills. Learning to give this care and attention to your writing will also have spin-offs in other areas of your thought and action. Do not be embarrassed to be a bit of a perfectionist. High achievers are all perfectionists in one way or another.

This means that when you have finished writing your essay, you probably have not finished work on it. You need to check and correct what you have written. Even if you took meticulous care as you wrote, you will still find errors and things you could improve when you read your work through again. Do not try to do this as soon as you finish writing. Give yourself a break from the project. If you have time, leave your essay overnight and come back to it the following day. If you are in more of a rush to finish, take a short break and do something that will clear your head. Have a shower, go out for a walk, have something to eat or drink, phone up a friend for a chat or watch something on the TV for half an hour. Any of these will help you to come back to your essay with fresh eyes so that you can start looking for things you can brush up.

If you are writing a long piece of work, such as a dissertation, you should plan to leave yourself several days, or even a week or two, for editing and correcting your work. If you can rope in a friend or relative to help you with this, so much the better. It is always harder to find errors in your own work, because your brain expects to see the words on the page the way that you intended them in the first place. A second reader will pick up more typos and slips of grammar than you will. However, they should not change or comment on the content of your essay.

punctuation matters

Punctuation matters. It does not simply tell the reader when to start and stop; it organizes the text into meaningful units, and shows the relationships between these units. Getting it wrong can seriously damage the sense of the text. On the other hand, getting it right can allow you to express your ideas with elegance and clarity. This chapter explains the basic rules for the most problematic punctuation marks: the apostrophe, the comma, the semi-colon, the colon, the dash and quotation marks. Each of these has a different function, and can help you to build strong, clear sentences. Learning to handle these confidently and correctly will sharpen up your writing, keep your marker happy, and will provide you with a highly-prized skill for the years beyond your course of study.

Apostrophes

The misuse of apostrophes is one of the most common problems in written English. You will see apostrophes in the wrong places in shops, theatre programmes, adverts, newspapers, restaurant menus and more. There is always some public debate going on about whether we should retain apostrophes in the language or abolish them because so few people seem capable of using them properly. However, the fact is that they still exist, and your tutors still expect you to be able to put them in the right places. Before writing this book, I asked my colleagues what they thought was the biggest problem in students' written work. Wrong use of apostrophes was overwhelmingly at the top of the list. The reason this annoys markers so much is that the rules are pretty simple. Here they are:

You can use an apostrophe:

* **to signal possession by adding 's to a singular noun: Susan's book, King's College, the boy's father, the woman's coat, the banana's skin.**

    If the noun or name already ends in **s** then go ahead and add **'s** as normal: **Tess's** book, **Dickens's** novels, the **bus's** driver. The exceptions to this are biblical and classical names ending in **s**, such as Jesus or Socrates, or names which already end with a 'ziz' sound: **Jesus'** name, **Socrates'** ideas, Mr **Bridges'** house.

    A plural noun ending in **s** takes an apostrophe after the **s**: the **boys'** fathers, the **ladies'** toilet, the **horses'** owner.

    A plural noun not ending in **s** takes **'s**: the **women's** rights, the **children's** school.

    Get into the habit of taking a moment to check if the apostrophe should be before or after the **s** every time you use one. Do not tuck the apostrophe into a name that already has an **s**: **Dicken's** novels, **Jame's** coat. Similarly, do not tuck an apostrophe into possessive pronouns (see below).

* **to signal a missing letter in a contraction such as don't, won't, isn't, it's.** However, these contractions are informal

and should not appear in academic essays, except when they appear in quotations from texts. Write out these phrases in full: **do not, will not, is not, it is.**

Do not use an apostrophe:
* **for plurals of nouns ending in vowels** such as **banana's, piano's, tomato's** instead of **bananas, pianos, tomatoes.** This is known as the 'greengrocer's apostrophe', but it crops up everywhere. There is no excuse for this; it is just plain wrong.
* **for possessive pronouns** such as **hers, yours, theirs, its, ours.** These are complete words, like **his** and **mine.**

It's and **its** are commonly confused, but this really annoys your marker, so get this one right. **It's** should never appear in your written work. If you mean **it is**, then write this out in full. If you mean **belonging to it,** then there is no apostrophe. Also look out for **who's** and **whose.**

Commas

Commas provide the internal structure of each sentence. They mark out which bits of the sentence are essential to its meaning and which bits are supplementary. They show where clauses start and stop, and they separate items in lists. Getting them in the right place keeps the movement of the sentence clear, but having too many can slow down your reader and make the sentence seem cluttered. Here are some rules which you should learn to observe:

You can use a comma:
* **to link two sentences with a conjunction (and, but, because, or).** This makes a compound sentence.
  ✓ I opened the book, and I began to read.
  I have chosen to link the two sentences with a comma and the word **and** to emphasize that I want the reader to take both sections as part of the same event. However, a comma cannot link two sentences by itself. If I insert a comma but miss out the word **and**, I create a comma splice. Technically it is possible to link together several sentences with commas

and conjunctions to make a very long, complex sentence. Novelists such as Virginia Woolf and Henry James do this all the time in their fiction, but you should avoid it. Limit yourself to one conjunction per sentence where possible. In essays, it is always better to write short, clear sentences.

* **after connective adverbs.** These words can be useful at the beginning of sentences in essays as they show how your argument is moving from sentence to sentence. **However, yet, still, nevertheless, therefore, thus, moreover, for example** and similar words are used to suggest a connection or contrast between two sentences without formally joining them. A comma is required after one of these when it appears at the beginning of a sentence.
  ✓ However, you will always make occasional mistakes.

However is particularly problematic. If you leave out this comma, it sounds like the whole sentence is a subordinate clause which should lead to some other statement. If **however** is operating as part of a subordinate clause, the comma goes after the clause:
  ✓ However much you try, you will always make occasional mistakes.

This is easy to get wrong, so look out for this one. There is more about clauses in the following chapter.

Though and **although** cannot be used as connective adverbs at the start of sentences:
  ✗ Although, many people try to do so.

They can, however, be used at the start of a subordinate clause:
  ✓ Although Elizabeth finds Darcy overbearing, she is obviously the only woman in the novel who is his intellectual equal.

* **to separate items in a list.** This works for nouns and adjectives:
  ✓ Oscar Wilde wrote novels, plays, poetry, journalism, criticism and children's stories. However, he is most famous for his colourful, controversial and self-destructive private life.

If you have three or more items, you should use **and** between the last two. Avoid listing verbs and adverbs. One at a time is quite enough.

* **to signal a parenthetical phrase.** Commas can be used like brackets to insert an extra piece of information, interesting or otherwise, into a sentence. Reread that last sentence without the words between the two commas. It still makes sense. The phrase between the commas is not a complete sentence. In this case it is a modifying phrase, which adds some extra information or comment about the preceding noun. The first comma signals a short diversion from the sentence. The second comma shows that this diversion is finished, and the sentence picks up where it left off. You could insert a different phrase or clause here, such as 'or even a witty aside', or 'if you have any extra information to insert'. Parenthetical phrases have great comic potential, but try to resist the temptation to use them in essays for hilarious remarks that probably will not seem so funny to your marker. Also avoid using them to include lists of things that you would like to mention but cannot be bothered to include properly in a working sentence:
  * ✗ Hamlet has many flaws, indecisiveness, arrogance, suspicion of others etc., which undermine his heroic potential.

  Here it would be better to say
  * ✓ Hamlet has many flaws which undermine his heroic potential. He is indecisive, arrogant and suspicious of others.

* **to mark out clauses.** If you are hazy about what a clause is, you need to read something that will explain the basics of grammar slowly and carefully. Traditional grammar marks every shift in the syntax of a sentence by inserting a comma. Modern writing is more relaxed about this. Some clauses do not need to be separated by commas, especially when a linking word, such as **that, whenever,** or **since,** is used to signal a relative clause. However, commas

can make a dramatic difference to the meaning of this kind of sentence. Leaving them out can make a sentence ambiguous.

* **to introduce speech.** A comma is used to introduce speech or a quotation when it forms part of the preceding or following sentence:

    ✓ Hamlet says, 'I know a hawk from a handsaw.'

    or

    ✓ 'I know a hawk from a handsaw,' says Hamlet.

    You can also use a colon to introduce a quotation or speech:

    ✓ Hamlet says: 'I know a hawk from a handsaw.'

* Always use a colon when the quotation follows a complete sentence:

    ✓ Hamlet insists that he is sane: 'I know a hawk from a handsaw.'

Do not use a comma:

* **to join sentences without a conjunction.** This creates a comma splice, which is next to dodgy apostrophes on the marker's hate list. A comma splice looks like this:

    ✘ Some markers are sent into a rage by comma splices, they will give themselves a hernia with fury, and will cover your essay in red pen.

    It should read:

    ✓ Some markers are sent into a rage by comma splices. They will give themselves a hernia with fury, and will cover your essay in red pen.

Semicolons

Few people know how to use a semicolon well, which is a pity, as this is an elegant element of style which can be used to create beautifully balanced sentences. It has two main functions in prose:

* **to connect two sentences.** This is a good antidote to the comma splice. It works especially well for short sentences where the sense follows on directly into the second sentence, and where the two halves are of equal importance and length:

✓ I opened the book; I began to read.

It is also possible to use a semicolon with a connective adverb:

✓ I opened the book; however, I did not begin to read.

This is more cumbersome and should be used sparingly.
The golden rule of using semicolons to join clauses is that
each half of the completed sentence should also operate
as a grammatical sentence in its own right. In other words,
only use a semicolon where you could put a full stop.

* **to separate items on a list.** This is especially useful when the
list is long and the individual items on the list include commas:

✓ Quantitative research has many strengths: it allows
researchers to consider a large number of responses,
thus giving a broad view of the issue; it encourages the
application of rigorous, systematic analysis; and it enables
researchers to observe shifting trends over a period of time.

This way the reader can easily tell where the important
divisions between the items occur. If this list only contained
commas, it would be very confusing. When using semicolons
in a list, it is a good idea to introduce the list with a colon to
show where the list begins.

Colons

Like semicolons, these are rarely used but are not as confusing
as many people think. The function of a colon is to introduce
information of some kind:

* **to introduce a list.** A colon announces that something
important is about to follow. This makes it ideal for kicking
off a long list, as above. The list can also be a sequence of
short items separated by commas:

✓ A cake requires four ingredients: flour, sugar, butter and eggs.

* **to introduce a quotation or speech.** This is very useful in
essays, and works well before a large, indented quotation.
Always use a colon to introduce a quotation which follows
a complete sentence. There are plenty of examples on these
pages.

* **to introduce an explanation or statement.** In this case the colon is used to create some sort of anticipation. It is often used when reporting speech or when summarizing or expanding the first half of the sentence:
  ✓ Austen's message is clear: money is an essential element in a happy marriage.
  or
  ✓ Elizabeth makes her feelings obvious: she despises Mr Collins.

Dashes

Unlike semicolons and colons, dashes are overused. They are often used by writers who are unsure which punctuation mark to choose. Dashes should not be used instead of brackets, parenthetical commas, semicolons, full stops or colons before lists and quotations. **Avoid** all of the following constructions:
  ✗ Elizabeth – an independent young woman – is in no hurry to marry.
  ✗ Elizabeth makes her feelings obvious – she despises Mr Collins.
  ✗ Elizabeth feels only one emotion for Mr Collins – contempt.

All of these can be rewritten using more appropriate punctuation. However, dashes do have their place, whatever some may say. When you use one make sure you type a long dash (–) not a short hyphen (-). Press Ctrl, Alt and the hyphen key at the top right of your keyboard. Alternatively, if you are working in a Word programme, you can type two short hyphens (--) without spaces between the two words on either side. When you hit the space bar at the end of the second word, the two hyphens will be converted to a long dash. Dashes are useful where the sense of the sentence is interrupted in some way, or where a long qualification or description has led away from the main point of the sentence. The dash provides a breathing space in which the sentence can reorganize itself:
  ✓ Elizabeth Bennett is young, attractive, intelligent, vivacious, independent to the point of stubbornness – the classic Austen heroine.

The final phrase does not fit easily into the syntax of the sentence, but it is obviously referring to the subject of the sentence, Elizabeth Bennett. If you were to put a comma after 'stubbornness', the final phrase would get lost in the list of adjectives. You could create a new sentence: 'She is the classic Austen heroine.' However, this lacks the immediacy and movement of the first version. A dash seems justified in this case.

Quotation marks

In British usage, speech and quotations are signalled by single quote marks:

✓ Dickens begins *A Christmas Carol* with a ghostly reference: 'Marley was dead: to begin with. There is no doubt whatever about that.'

Quotations and speech within quotations are signalled by double quote marks:

✓ '"Bah!" said Scrooge, "Humbug!"'

You will see this done the other way around, with double quote marks on the outside and single quotes within. This will probably be in books or journals published in the US, where the system is reversed. Please use the system of the country where you are writing.

If you have quoted a complete sentence, put any punctuation inside the quotation marks. This shows that the quote is complete in itself. For example:

✓ She said, 'This essay is very well written.'

If you have quoted a part of a sentence, put the punctuation outside the quotation marks. This shows that the quote needs the rest of the sentence to make sense:

✓ She said that the essay was 'very well written'.

In US usage punctuation always goes inside quotation marks.

*make
sentences
make sense*

Language needs grammar. It is essential if you want to construct any kind of statement beyond simply naming objects. If you want to express interesting ideas then a sound grasp of grammar is required. Some students manage to use grammar well enough most of the time without knowing all the terms for the techniques they are using. This is fine when it works, but if you do not know the vocabulary of grammar it can be hard to stand back and analyse where a sentence went wrong. Markers tend to employ technical, grammatical terms when pointing out problems in your work, which is not much use to you if you do not know what they are talking about. This chapter will highlight a few common problems, and offer definitions of terms that may crop up in your markers' comments.

Clauses

Clauses are the internal sections of a sentence, which fit together to build up meaning. Every clause has a noun and a verb or, if you prefer, a thing and an action. These are sometimes called the subject and the predicate. However, not all clauses are of equal weight and value. The clauses of a sentence are like the internal walls of a house. Some can be moved around or altered without doing too much damage. One is always essential and cannot be removed without the whole thing falling in. Clauses which are essential are **main clauses.** A compound sentence will have two main clauses. A main clause requires a noun and a verb:

I know.

However, it can also be more elaborate:

I know some useful things about grammar.

A main clause is the part of a sentence which can make a sentence all by itself. 'Know' is the **principal verb** of this sentence, which means it is the verb in the main clause. 'I' is the **subject** of the sentence. This means it is the noun doing the verb, also called the **predicate.** 'Some useful things about grammar' forms the **object** of the sentence. This is the noun phrase which represents the thing that 'I know'. Subjects, objects and predicates can all be made up of single words or phrases to make up a main clause.

Subordinate clauses

On to this main clause you can attach other clauses which support and describe the main clause. These are called **subordinate clauses.** All the subordinate clauses in the following examples are in bold. Subordinate clauses can often be moved around without changing the meaning of a sentence:

I know some useful things about grammar, **which is lucky for you.**

or

It is lucky for you that I know some useful things about grammar.

A subordinate clause is a section of a sentence which contains a subject and a predicate (i.e. a noun and a verb), but which is doing the job of an adverb or an adjective. It is not part of the main action of the sentence. It is describing a thing or an action in the main clause or in another subordinate clause. A sentence can have more than one subordinate clause. They can follow and/or precede the main clause.

Because I have studied English, I know some useful things about grammar, **which is lucky for you, as you can draw on these to improve your writing.**

By now, however, this sentence is getting a bit long and complex for my liking. Once you have more than three clauses in a sentence, it is very easy to get muddled up about which is the important one. I advise against sentences any more complex than this. They are hard to write well and hard work to read. The real danger is that the main clause is missed out, and you end up with something like this:

✗ **Because I have studied English, which is lucky for you, as you can draw on these to improve your writing.**

This is not a sentence. It has no main verb, only a succession of subordinate clauses. A subordinate clause is often flagged up by a word such as **while, which, if, that, whenever, although, as, despite.** This kind of clause describes the subject, the object or the predicate of the main clause. A phrase containing a **participle** (usually a verb ending in **-ing**) behaves similarly. These cannot form sentences in their own right, so you should avoid things such as this:

✗ Although this is not the case.
✗ However much you try.
✗ Rarely appearing to do so.
✗ Being of sound mind and judgement.

All of these are **sentence fragments.** They do have nouns and verbs, but they lack a principal verb and are not valid as stand-alone sentences in formal written English. They have no place in academic essays. The Microsoft grammar check will not always pick up sentence fragments, so you need to correct these carefully yourself.

Dangling elements

You also need to make sure that the different parts of the sentence match up in a way that makes sense. A subordinate clause or participle phrase at the start of a sentence is known as a **hanging clause.** This can cause complications when it is not quite clear to which bit of the main clause it refers. For example:

> **While she was writing** *The Voyage Out*, Virginia Woolf's sister Vanessa Bell painted her portrait.

This particular type of hanging clause is called a **dangling clause,** because it dangles ambiguously from the main clause, which it should modify and clarify. This sentence suggests that Virginia Woolf's sister wrote *The Voyage Out*, which is not the case. It also fails to make clear whose portrait was painted. In this sort of sentence, try to keep the subject of the main clause as the subject of the subordinate clause, so that the two halves of the sentence are talking about the same thing or person. This may require some rewording:

> While Virginia Woolf was writing *The Voyage Out*, she sat for a portrait painted by her sister Vanessa Bell.

Relative clauses

A relative clause is a subordinate clause which refers to a preceding noun or pronoun. It usually starts with **who, which** or **that**:

> The play **which we studied last year** is out of print.

Relative clauses can be divided into two:
A **defining relative clause** is essential to the meaning of the sentence because it gives important information about the preceding word. This identifies it in some way, marking it out from all other possible occurrences of the word. The example above is a defining relative clause. It makes clear that the sentence is

discussing one particular play studied last year, in contrast to any other plays studied this year or two years ago.

A **non-defining relative clause** offers information that describes but does not specify; it is doing the same job as a modifying clause in a parenthesis. Like this, it must be enclosed in commas to keep it out of the way of the main action of the sentence:

✓ Shakespeare, **who was born in 1564,** wrote poetry as well as plays.

When the clause defines, there are no commas. When it does not, it is surrounded by commas, or by a comma and a full stop, if it ends the sentence. Remember to add the second comma after a non-defining relative clause. Avoid things like this:

✗ Shakespeare, who was born in 1564 wrote poetry as well as plays.

It is important to decide whether a relative clause is defining or non-defining, because the commas alone can change the meaning completely. Compare the two pairs of sentences below:

He answered all the questions which were on Shakespeare.

or

He answered all the questions, which were on Shakespeare.

Were all the available questions on Shakespeare or not? How many did he answer? My personal favourite in this category is:

All the sailors who were in the lifeboat were saved.

or

All the sailors, who were in the lifeboat, were saved.

The first sentence implies that some sailors did not make it into the lifeboat and came to a sorry end. The other one says that all the sailors were in the lifeboat and survived. Who says that punctuation is not a matter of life and death?

Pronouns

Pronouns are the words in a sentence which do the job of filling in for a noun or a noun phrase which could be there instead. For example, take a sentence with three nouns:

The boy handed **the book** to **the girl**.

Any of these nouns can be substituted for a pronoun.

He handed the book to the girl.
He handed **it** to the girl.
He handed **it** to **her**.

Remember that pronouns can also fill in for proper names, abstract ideas, or groups of people and things. Any noun can be replaced with a pronoun. When you are constructing a sentence with one or more pronouns, try to bear in mind what each of the pronouns is representing and make this clear to your reader. This can help you to avoid some basic errors.

Which noun is it?

A pronoun always refers to the most recent plausible noun. This is called the **law of antecedents**. It works like this:

The cat dropped the mouse. It ran away.

This says that the mouse ran away, not the cat. However, a gendered pronoun will match up with the most recent gendered noun, or proper name.

The girl dropped the mouse. She ran away.

In this case it is the girl who runs away. Technically, of course, it might be a female mouse. However, we are not told the mouse's gender, so the girl is the most likely candidate for **she**.

Pronouns can get out of hand when there are too many of them in a sentence, especially if the sentence contains an indefinite pronoun or two, such as **it** and **this.** For example, what does this mean?

It is useful to note that Hamlet's indecision about killing his uncle takes more time than it should, but this does not mean that it is morally wrong, and this might be the case because he is able to think about it first.

Is it Hamlet's indecision or the killing of his uncle that may or may not be wrong? What might be the case? Who is able to think about it first: Hamlet or his uncle? A student who writes a sentence like this may have an idea in their own head what they mean, but they have not exactly made their point clear. On the whole, you should avoid starting sentences with **it** and **this** whenever possible, and be aware that pronouns used later in a sentence may be misread if not clearly attached to an earlier noun. When editing, always strike out pointless phrases such as 'it is useful to note that'. Write shorter, clearer sentences.

I and me

In speech and in writing, people are often confused about the difference between **I** and **me**, especially if these are paired up with another noun. For example:

   ✗ **Me** and my sister went to town.
   ✗ The taxi came to collect my sister and I.

This happens because there has been a mix-up about which pronoun is the subject of the sentence. You should use **I** as the subject of the sentence. When **I** is the person doing the action, then **I** is the subject of the sentence. You should use **me** as the object of the sentence. When something happens to **me**, then **me** is the object of the sentence. This remains the same whether there is an extra person added in or not. You would not say:

   ✗ **Me** went to town.

or

   ✗ The taxi came to collect **I**.

So the correct usage is:

   ✓ My sister and **I** went to town.

and

✓ The taxi came to collect my sister and **me**.

Who and whom

Many writers have a similar problem with **who** and **whom**. **Who** should be used when the noun that **who** represents is the subject of the sentence or clause in which it appears. **Whom** should be used when the noun it represents is the object of the sentence or clause. For example:

✗ I have a brother **whom** lives in London.

✗ **Who** does this belong to?

For some reason most people have a lot less trouble with this issue in relation to **he** and **she**, or **him** and **her**. So you can use these pronouns to work out whether you need **who** or **whom**. Rethink the sentence with a personal pronoun and you will be able to decide whether it is a subject or an object:

✓ **He** lives in London.

✓ This belongs to **her**.

He, she and **I** are all subject pronouns, so replace these with **who**.

✓ I have a brother **who** lives in London.

Him, her and **me** are all object pronouns, so replace these with **whom**.

✓ **Whom** does this belong to?

This example includes a preposition: **to.** Prepositions are words which tell you the relationship of one noun or pronoun to another. It can help to think of these as placing words which tell you where things are, for example: **in, with, by, from, up, at, on.** Prepositions are often clues that you should be using **whom** rather than **who**. For example: **to whom, by whom, with whom, from whom.** It will be easier to work out whether you need **who** or **whom** if you organize the sentence so that the preposition and the pronoun stay together:

✓ To **whom** does this belong?

Spelling

There is no short cut to good spelling. You just have to learn what each word in the language looks like. However, there is one simple thing you can do which will help: buy a dictionary. A good dictionary will be the most useful book you buy during your time as a student, so do not begrudge the money for it. There is no point spending a week's rent on a leather-bound, two-volume, deluxe dictionary. Buy a small, compact dictionary, ideally less than 20 cm tall, that is light enough and sturdy enough to travel in your rucksack. A dictionary on the bookshelf at home is no use if you are working in the library or the computing centre. Get into the habit of taking your dictionary with you when you are writing, and look up words you are unsure about. This will not just help with your spelling; make sure that you also read and understand the definition of the words you use. It is easy to confuse similar words. Using a dictionary rather than the spellcheck on your PC can help you avoid some embarrassing errors.

10

making sources work

Effective use of source material is crucial if you want to produce really good written work. Chapter 4 discussed where to find good resources for your project. However, selecting and reading good source material is only part of using sources well. This chapter explores a few strategies for using your material to form judgements and strengthen your argument. It also looks at the kind of language you should use when discussing other scholars' work and gives some advice about avoiding plagiarism. Remember that the active use of sources is integral to constructing a strong essay. You don't just want to keep on the right side of the regulations and to create an impressive list of references. You also want to show off your knowledge, engage with an interesting debate in your subject area and use your sources to back up your own ideas.

It is almost impossible to write a really good essay or dissertation without some use of secondary sources. If you are presenting a report of your own research project, you will need to demonstrate that you have looked at relevant scholarship. If you are constructing a formal essay or a literature review, then source material will probably form the central element of your project. Even if you are writing a critical analysis or a learning log, which may not call for direct use of secondary sources, you will produce a better piece of work if you have a good knowledge of a range of background material and recent scholarship in your area of study. Learning from other thinkers and writers is what studying is all about, and reading other people's work can sharpen up your own ideas. However, you need to know how to incorporate other writers' work into your own. Good use of secondary material shows that you have done your research, and that you are confident about your own opinions. Effective use of source material is often the factor that distinguishes a first-class essay from a high second-class one.

Use your secondary material to set up a debate within your essay or dissertation. Scholarly literature provides an opportunity for scholars to test out their own ideas and to challenge other people's. Academic journals and publishers host some fiercely fought debates about all kinds of subjects. Try to give a flavour of the cut and thrust of debate in your own discipline in your work.

You are much more likely to create a strong argument if you include some material which presents a perspective opposed to your own, especially if you can show that perspective to be in some way flawed. Students often discard any secondary material with which they disagree and then wonder why their marker complains about an essay that is 'flat' or 'short on analysis'. This is like taking the springs out of a trampoline and then wondering why it does not bounce. If you come across any material that you can prove is missing the point, roll up your sleeves and get to work on it. Just make sure you can back up your position with material from your primary texts, your own research findings or from other scholars. Sometimes pure logic will do the trick too. This is the sort of thing that really makes an essay shine. So, be assertive with experts. They are only human after all.

Always acknowledge your sources actively. Do not rely on your footnotes and references to make your essay make sense. That is not their job. Make it absolutely clear who said what, and whether you and other scholars agree. Your essay will read much more coherently.

Layout of quotations

It is important to present your quoted material neatly, so that your marker can see clearly where quotations start and stop. The rules for quoting primary and secondary material are the same. However, the format of your quote may vary depending on the length of the quote and the type of material you are quoting.

* **Short quotations:** Quotations of a few words should be incorporated into a sentence:
    * ✓ Pip's 'great expectations' prove to be not at all what he imagines.

    or

    * ✓ Joe's repeated phrase, 'what larks', represents his lack of education as well as his affectionate, boyish relationship with Pip.[1]

* **Quotations of up to 40 words:** These may also be incorporated into your text. They should be preceded by a colon or comma when appropriate:
    * ✓ Charles Dickens sets Pip's story in a landscape similar to that of his own childhood: 'Ours was the marsh country, down by the river, within, as the river wound, twenty miles of the sea.'

    The colon or comma is not needed if a word such as **that, which,** or **whether** introduces the quotation. In this case, the quotation functions as a subordinate clause, and is an integral part of the wider sentence. When the quotation appears within a sentence, the final full stop should appear

[1] Charles Dickens, *Great Expectations* (1861; repr. London: Everyman, 1994), p. 193.

outside the quotation marks, even if the full stop is part of the original sentence. A page number in brackets should go inside the full stop when the quotation is run on in the text:

✓ Charles Dickens sets Pip's story in a landscape similar to that of his own childhood. Pip tells the reader that 'Ours was the marsh country, down by the river, within, as the river wound, twenty miles of the sea' (Dickens, p.1).

or

✓ Pip believes Miss Havisham is the source of his 'great expectations'.

* **Quotations of more than 40 words:** These should be set apart in an indented paragraph of their own. Leave a line, indent the whole paragraph one tab space from the margin, and set out the passage **without** quotation marks, except for those that may appear in the passage quoted:

✓ Charles Dickens sets Pip's story in a landscape similar to that of his own childhood. He quickly connects Pip's identity with this landscape and with the day on which he meets Magwitch:

> Ours was the marsh country, down by the river, within, as the river wound, twenty miles of the sea. My first most vivid and broad impression of the identity of things, seems to me to have been gained on a memorable raw afternoon towards evening. (Dickens, p.1)

Footnote numbers and subsequent page references in brackets should appear after the full stop for indented quotes. After an indented quote there is no need to indent the first line of text, unless you intend to start a new paragraph.

To signal that you have omitted a short section of a quote use ellipses in square brackets [...]. The brackets signal that these ellipses are yours:

✓ At such a time I found out for certain [...] that the low leaden line beyond was the river; and that the distant savage lair from which the wind was rushing, was the sea; and that the small bundle of shivers growing afraid of it all and beginning to cry, was Pip. (Dickens, p.1)

Make sure that the quote still makes grammatical sense in its own right. You must also make sure that you do not corrupt the meaning of the author's original sentence. Only use ellipses to travel a short distance within a text. Use it to join sections of the same sentence, or possibly adjoining sentences. If you wish to quote clauses or phrases that are further apart, do so in two separate quotations. Do not use ellipses to indicate a large section of text which all seems relevant, but which you cannot be bothered to sift through for important phrases or sentences:

> ✗ Charles Dickens sets Pip's story in a landscape similar to that of his own childhood. He quickly connects Pip's identity with this landscape and with the day on with he meets Magwitch: 'My father's family [...] beginning to cry, was Pip' (Dickens, p.1).

Plagiarism

Plagiarism is viewed as a serious offence in the academic world and can lead to a student being thrown out of their college or university. There are many different forms of plagiarism, but the basic idea remains the same: **plagiarism is the use of the intellectual work of another person without due acknowledgement.** Academics do not just regard plagiarism as laziness or cheating. They see it as a form of stealing. Academics make their living by having ideas. If you use these ideas without giving credit for them, it is a bit like having a meal in a restaurant without paying. There are three main forms of plagiarism in student essays:

1 quoting a source verbatim (word-for-word) without quotation marks as though you had written it yourself
2 using an idea which you have read, but failing to reference it, thus giving the impression that it was your own brilliant idea
3 copying the work of another student and submitting it as your own work.

None of these is allowed under any circumstances.

Since the advent of the internet, most of us have become used to the idea that we can get any information we want, whenever we want it, and for any purpose we want at the touch of a button. We have also all become much better at cutting and pasting material from here and there to draw together lots of information in a hurry. However, if you still think you can write your academic essays like this, you had better go back and start reading this book all over again. A good essay is much more than a patchwork of sources tacked together. It should be a well-thought-out argument which balances source materials with your own opinions and findings.

Remember that when you are writing an essay you are not just trying to reach the right answer, you are trying to show your marker the skills that you used to arrive at your answer, and the research that helped you get there. A large part of this is being careful and transparent about all the sources that you use. All your information should be traceable back to a reliable source. Tutors are usually keen for students to explore interesting and unusual sources of information, but you must show where you found your information. Plagiarism is the deliberate failure to do this.

If you have copied something, even a short phrase, word for word out of a book, or if you have copied and pasted anything from an internet site or e-text, you must put it in quotation marks and give a reference. Changing one or two words, or paraphrasing a sentence does not release you from the obligation to name your sources. Look at the two versions of the same paragraph below. The first one is clearly plagiarizing. The second one shows where the ideas and the language really came from:

- ✓ Hamlet is reluctant to kill his uncle in revenge for his father's murder, but this may be connected to a repressed sexual attraction to his mother. So it is possible that his hesitancy is due to some special cause of repugnance for his task, even if he is unaware of the nature of this repugnance.

- ✓ Ernest Jones argues that Hamlet's reluctance to kill his uncle can all the traced back to his repressed desire for his mother. He claims that Hamlet's confusion about his feelings towards his father and uncle are due to his jealousy at their relationships with Gertrude. However, this theory seems implausible, as Hamlet clearly loves and reveres his father, a detail which Jones fails to fit into his Freudian reading.

This makes it clear which ideas are Jones's and which are original.

If you are ever tempted to cut a corner or two with a quick bit of quote-lifting, just remember this: your marker is quite smart. With a few rare exceptions, markers know more about the subject than you do, have a good idea of the kind of source material you might come across, and have seen a lot of essays at your level of work. They may also have a good idea of how capable you are, and of the type of work which you are likely to submit. If there is something out of place about your essay, they will be on to it in a flash.

11

referencing

Good referencing demonstrates that you care about the accuracy and the reliability of your sources. It shows where your ideas come from, keeps you on the right side of the plagiarism rules, and allows your reader to refer back to your material if required. It also shows that you are attentive to details, which gives your argument more authority. People are always more willing to listen to your big ideas if you can get the small things right. So, referencing is a good chance to practise taking care with facts and figures, which is another skill that you will find useful in all sorts of contexts. This chapter gives an introduction to the two main styles of referencing: the author–date system and footnotes. Find out which style is standard for your subject, and consider investing in a style guide which can give you further advice in this area.

Using the author–date system

The author–date system is an excellent referencing system to use if your subject calls for a thorough knowledge of recent scholarly publications such as journal articles. This style makes it easy to refer to relevant scholarship in your text, even if you have not quoted it directly. It also makes the publication date of this scholarship very visible, which is often important.

When you quote material from a source or when you refer to an argument or information from an article or book, you should give an author–date reference in brackets in the main body of your text. Try to place this reference close to the relevant material without spoiling the shape of your sentence. References should be given in the following format:

(Author's surname, date of publication)

For example:

(Bernard, 2000)

If you have quoted directly from the text, you should also give a page number:

(Smith, 1983, p.6)

If you use the author's name in the text, you only need to give the date. Here is an example of a paragraph which includes several author–date references:

Quantitative researchers have in the past been caricatured as 'number-crunchers' (Smith, 1983, p.6). However, in recent years, more mixed-method approaches have developed in social-science research. For example, researchers using surveying techniques recognize the importance of social interaction as part of the survey process (Bernard, 2000), while researchers using ethnographic approaches are also learning to adopt statistical and inductive methods (Cloke et al., 2004). Ackroyd and Hughes (1992) point out that whatever methods are used, the research should always be systematic and rigorous.

At the end of the essay you should include a reference list, sometimes called a 'works cited' list, which contains the full bibliographic references to all of your sources. You can divide this into primary and secondary sources, if appropriate. However, you should not create separate sections for books, journals or other types of source material. Present your list in alphabetical order of the author's surname. The author's name and initials should be reversed to make this order clear. If there are two authors, place the item in the list according to the surname of the first author. You should also reverse the name and initials of all the authors. The format of the reference will vary slightly depending on the type of publication. Take special care to get the punctuation right.

Books

Put book titles in italics or underline them. Whichever you choose, you should be consistent. List books using the following format:

Author (date) *title of book in italics*. Place of publication: publisher.

For example:

Bernard, H. R. (2000) *Social Research Methods: Qualitative and Quantitative Approaches*. London: Sage Publications.

Chapters in edited books

Titles of chapters or articles in edited books should be given in quotation marks. When you reference a book chapter in the text, give the name of the author of the chapter and the publication date. In the reference list, cite the chapter first, followed by the reference information for the book. The name of an editor or translator is not reversed:

Author of article (date) 'title of article'. *In* editor of book, ed. *title of book*. Place of publication: publisher, pp. xx–xx.

For example:

Conklin, H.C. (1968) 'Ethnography'. *In* D. L. Sills, ed.
International Encyclopedia of the Social Sciences.
New York: Macmillan, pp. 172–8.

Articles in journals

Titles of articles should also be given in quotation marks.
Titles of journals are given in italics like book titles. Give the
information for the article, followed by the information for the
journal:

Author (date) 'title of article in quotation marks'.
Title of journal in italics, **volume no (part volume no.),**
pp. xx–xx.

For example:

Smith, J. K. (1983) 'Quantitative versus Qualitative
Research: An Attempt to Clarify the Issue'. *Educational*
Researcher, **12 (3), pp.6–13.**

Electronic journals

Online journals should be cited in the same format as print
journals. However, you should also add the url address of the article
and the date on which you accessed the article:

Author (date), 'title of article'. *Title of journal*, **volume**
number (and part), pp. xx–xx. <url address>
[Accessed date].

For example:

Van Wienen, M. (1995) 'Poetics of the Frugal Housewife:
A Modernist Narrative of the Great War and
America'. *American Literary History*, **7 (1), pp. 55–91.**
http://links.jstor.org **[Accessed 28 March 2011].**

Websites

If you are referencing online material that is not published as a journal article you should give as much of the following information as you can find:

Author (date), 'title of article'. *Title of web publication*. (Date of publication) place of publication: publisher. <url address> [Accessed date].

For example:

Cornwall, N. (2006), 'The Aspern Papers'. *The Literary Encyclopedia*. (17 Jan 2006). The Literary Dictionary Company. http://www.litencyc.com/php/sworks. php?rec=true&UID=1559 [Accessed 28 March 2011].

Referencing with footnotes

Footnotes are an excellent way of referencing material if your subject involves working closely with textual material.

The following pages give advice on the MHRA system, which is based on footnotes. The first time you mention a text, give a footnote. If you mention the same text later in your essay, do not give a footnote. Give a short reference in brackets within your text: (Dickens, p.67). If you are using more than one text by the same author it might be less confusing to give a short version of the title or an abbreviation: (*Great Ex*, p.67) or (*GE*, p.67).

The format is slightly different for books, articles and websites. The rules are given below. Make sure you copy the punctuation as well. Footnotes should always have a full stop. At the end of your essay you should also include a bibliography.

Books

On first reference to a book, you should give a footnote in this format:

Author's name, *title of book in italics* (place of publication: publisher, date), p.x or pp. xx–xx.

For example:

Bella Bathurst, *The Lighthouse Stevensons* (London: HarperCollins, 2000), p.23.

Articles or essays in books

Titles of articles or essays are placed in quotation marks to indicate that they are not book titles. Give the details of the article, followed by the details of the book in which it appears, including the editor, if there is one. Give the page numbers for the complete article, followed by the page number for your quotation:

Author's name, 'title of article', in *title of book*, ed. by editor's name (place: publisher, date), page numbers, p.x.

For example:

Philip Horne, 'Henry James and the Invention of Novel Theory', in *The Cambridge Companion to Henry James*, ed. by Jonathan Freedman (Cambridge: Cambridge University Press, 1998), 79–101, p.85.

Articles in journals

These follow a similar format, but the information about editor, place of publication and publisher is not necessary. The title of the article appears in quotation marks. The title of the journal or newspaper appears in italics. For journals give the issue number followed by the year:

Author's name, 'title of article', *title of journal*, volume number (date), page numbers, p.x.

For example:

Lorna J. Philip, 'Planned Villages in South-west Scotland, 1730–1855; Analysing Functional Characteristics', *Landscapes*, 6 (1), 83–107, p.101.

Websites

Give as much of the following information as you can find:

Author, 'title of article', place of publication: publisher, (date). <url address> [Accessed date].

For example:

S. N. Clarke, 'Virginia Woolf: A Short Biography', Virginia Woolf Society of Great Britain, (2000). http://www.virginiawoolfsociety. co.uk/vw_res.biography.htm [Accessed 28 March 2011].

Short stories

As with essays and articles, short-story titles are placed in quotation marks to indicate that they are not book titles. Give the details of the short story, followed by the details of the book in which it appears, including the editor, if there is one. Give the page numbers for the complete story, followed by the page number for your quotation:

Author's name, 'title of short story', in *title of book*, ed. by editor's name (place: publisher, date), page numbers, p.x.

For example:

Vernon Lee, 'Winthrop's Adventure', in *The Virago Book of Victorian Ghost Stories*, ed. by Richard Dalby (London: Virago, 1988), 105–34, p.127.

Bibliography

At the end of every essay give a bibliography. List works from which you have quoted or which have informed your thinking, even if you have only included one or two texts. Do not list works which you have not read or which you glanced at briefly. If you are working on a project which involved primary source material, divide the bibliography into primary texts and secondary texts. In MHRA style, references in a bibliography follow the same format as footnotes with two exceptions:

1 The surname of the author is placed first, so that the items can easily be put into alphabetical order.
2 A bibliographic reference does not have a full stop.

Conclusion

This book has given you the key skills you need to tackle any piece of written work. Of course, there is still more that you can learn and, as you apply what you have read in these pages, you will create your own strategies for handling problem areas in your own subject. As you develop your skills, remember a few basic principles:

* **Think big.** Think about the skills you are acquiring, the degree you are taking and the subject you are studying. Learn to see your written work as part of the broader process of your education in a wide and fascinating subject.

* **Pay attention to details.** Take care with the little elements of language and layout that are easy to overlook. Attention to detail is the sign of a thorough and hard-working mind. It is a very good habit to form, and can help you develop into a more precise thinker.

* **Make life easy for your marker.** Always remember that essays look rather different when you have a pile of 20 to mark for the following day. Give your marker something that is neatly presented and a pleasure to read. It can only help.

* **Enjoy what you write.** Studying should not be a chore. Learn to love the language, and use it with focus and style.

You will never regret the time you spend learning to write well. It is a skill that you will find useful for the rest of your life.

Notes

Notes

Notes

Notes